Set Free

Kingdom Principles for Living Victoriously

John 6:40 — "And this is the will of Him who sent Me, that everyone who sees the Son and believes in Him may have everlasting life…"

Book 3

Nancy Williams

Way of Life Publishing

Nancy Williams
Copyright © 2009 by Nancy Williams
Revised 2016, 2023

No part of this book may be reproduced or transmitted in any form or by any means, electronic or mechanical, including photocopying and recording, or by any information storage or retrieval system except as may be expressly permitted in writing by the author. Permission requests are to be addressed in writing at AWayofLifeMinistries.com. All scripture quotations, unless otherwise indicated, are from the New King James Version.

ISBN: **979-8-9875825-2-7**

PRINTED IN THE UNITED STATES OF AMERICA

To order additional copies of this resource

Visit: AWayofLifeMinistries.com, Barnes and Noble & Amazon.com

E-book available

DEDICATION

To those who read this:

> This is dedicated to you, in the hopes that through this book you will find a deeper meaning in your walk with Christ. I hope a living Christianity will be yours. That you feel how much you are loved; that you see more clearly how the Bible applies to you; and that you will then embrace and incorporate these principles into your way of being and living.

I want to thank and acknowledge my loving husband, Jaycee, and daughter, Natalie, for lovingly and graciously supporting me as I took time away to complete this labor of love.

PREMISE FOR THIS WORK

Based on Romans 3:23, where God says that all have sinned and fall short of the glory of God, it is this book's premise that all of us require healing. We believe it is through sin, starting with Adam and Eve and passed down from generation to generation, that dysfunctional patterns began. It is sin that separates us from God, says Isaiah 59:2.

It is our goal to facilitate:

    1st — Looking at ourselves honestly

    2nd — Accepting God's grace, love and truth so that

    3rd — We can be set free from our sins

We propose to do this by using God's Word and following His way.

We believe the fruit of this will be:

- An intimate relationship with God the Father, God the Son and God the Holy Spirit
- The abundant life from God will be ours as we live and grow in this dynamic relationship
- Manifestation of the gifts of the Spirit in us which is for the profit of all and that God gives as He sees fit and when He sees fit (1 Corinthians 12:7-11). These gifts of the spirit include:
    a. Word of wisdom
    b. Word of knowledge

c. Faith

d. Gift of healing

e. Working of miracles

f. Gift of prophecy

g. Discerning of spirits

h. Gift of tongues

i. Interpretation of tongues

HOW TO USE THESE CHAPTERS

Bringing sinful patterns to the surface and dealing with them according to God's principles will restore your path in life and repair the breach separating you from others and from God, as stated in Isaiah 58:12. Individuals who have gone through this book have found the Holy Spirit and stated that they were empowered and enabled to trust God and look honestly at their lives.

God calls you and all of us to live a principled life. As you incorporate His principles in this book, the Holy Spirit will naturally flow through you to others. This book will cover 3 of God's principles as well as a growth plan and emphasizes God's principles, as found in the Bible, as the only source of living victoriously. As God created the world and set up universal principles by which it operates, relational principles are found within this creation and the Bible. He and His principles are the source of life and as you incorporate them, your life will flow smoother with less turmoil and more success. Therefore, memorize some of the given scriptures and the Holy Spirit will bring them to your remembrance in your time of need. "God's Word will not return void" (Isaiah 55:11). You will be affected by memorizing His Word even if you do not feel that an impact is being made. In each chapter, answer the questions to the best of your ability and you will be amazed at what starts happening within you!

This work is divided into 4 books which can be completed separately or sequentially by yourself or within a group setting.

If going through A Way of Life in a group setting, the facilitator may decide to share a short weekly teaching which provides the biblical foundation for the principle/s being reviewed, such as confession or repentance. The main group could then be divided into groups with a group facilitator present to promote sharing what God is doing in each other's lives, what the chapter review has brought to light and any hindrance in depending on God. The main facilitator may bring the whole group back together at the end for sharing and prayer or each group could end their time with prayer.

Additional supportive subjects are found in the appendix at the back of each book in this series of 4.

And now, let us continue with discovering and applying God's Kingdom Principles for Living Victoriously!

INTRODUCTION

Looking at being a disciple of God's kingdom principles and learning of and following the leading of the Holy Spirit is what this book will walk you through. With Book 3, you will learn about what it means to repent, what forgiveness is and isn't and how best to reconcile past relationships and hurts. Forgiveness of yourself and others releases the chains that bind and is where you are set free. I am excited for you! Stay the course. It's not always easy but it's worth it.

Let's start this book looking at your identity as a child of the Most High God. ☺

You are created in the image of God and hence, are very valuable and precious in His sight and loved unconditionally. You also have a purpose that you were born to fulfill and as you draw close to God and His way, you will become aware of and can then live out what was ordained for you from the beginning of time.

The Westminster Catechism states, in question 1 with the answer:

- "Q. 1. What is the chief end of man?
- Man's chief end is to glorify God and to enjoy him forever. 1 Cor. 10:31; Rom. 11:36; Ps. 73:25-28."

So, your goal is to get to know God and enjoy Him and as you do that (and in spite of), He enjoys you as well!

Before beginning, it's important to evaluate how you show up in life and look at how Jesus showed up, as He is our example to follow. You might be saying to yourself, "What is meant by how you show up?" In relationships with others, this means, are your moods and spirit happy, anxious, sad, overbearing, funny, serious, demanding, irritating, or goofy, to name a few. It's what you dole or give out to others and their experience of you. Jesus showed up with tough yet unconditional love for others and knew their heart motives and feelings. The way He showed up was compassionate and He listened well. Jesus could tell when some of the religious leaders were trying to trick Him and called them out about it. His heart was one for them to understand the will of His Father and for them to hear Him, but the religious rulers did not. Those that did, allowed Him to change them from the inside out as they got revelation or understanding about what love truly is and how God calls us to act, or *be, from the inside out.*

WHAT DOES IT MEAN TO BE?

You might have heard well-meaning messages about loving one another and treating each other with compassion and kindness while doing what's right. And yet, this message misses the mark. You might attempt to *put on* these character traits rather than *be* them on the inside and then wonder why results are not evident. Loving, authentic Christianity is not the witness. So why is this? God created you to *be* love and when you are not, there's no authenticity nor behaving from the core of who you were created to be.

Here's your example:

1. Jesus was and is love
2. Jesus loved

Jesus came from an unconditional, divine state of being so He could then love in human flesh. Then and only then, could He manifest in power, effect and results. He chose to *be* love and is love. The difference is becoming love (a noun) on the inside instead of attempting to put it on and act loving on the outside when you aren't that on the inside. You may attempt to be what you are not which is what Jesus came to change. Transformation is the process and freedom is the result. Free to be who you were created to be!

So, like Jesus, you are to live and *be*, powered by the choice to love and be love. Being love is by choice, intention and commitment, empowered by His Holy Spirit. When you choose love and allow the Holy Spirit to guide you, you are your authentic self.

Remember, others live with you and maybe even more important, you live with yourself. The million-dollar question is, "How do you want to live with yourself?" Would you want to be the type of person who is open, calm, joyful, authentic, honest and loving, or the opposite? If you want the former, you get to choose to follow the example Jesus gave you of unconditional, authentic love. Then abundant life can flow through you to others and this life can be true, pure and lovely. When you are unconditional love, you are truly free.

> Free to fly to the music of His joy,
> Free to feel the waves tumble us in playfulness,
> Free Choice—
> The way it is meant to be.

THE HOLY SPIRIT

In this world, the war against good and evil is extremely evident. On one side is the good side, with peace and harmony. The other side is dark, which is evil. There is a call on the dark side to all who will hear to succumb to the pull of power, anger, death and destruction. This evil pull is so strong that it separates families, friends and even those in power.

God, in the person of the Holy Spirit, is a counselor and giver of knowledge and wisdom. God, in the person of the Holy Spirit, will come into your heart to be your guide and strength if you ask Him to! How this works will be covered throughout the rest of this book.

There are good and evil forces at work around you, ALL the time. You may or may not be aware of the evil temptations that pull you to do wrong things. To become a warrior of God, this work will support you in becoming more aware as well as increasing your connection with the Holy Spirit. You will learn how the Holy Spirit can guide you into all truth and warn you of danger, to list a few of the works He does!

As an example of how the Holy Spirit may talk to you, I will share an experience I had where the Holy Spirit gave me a gift of knowledge. At a church I was attending, I was on the prayer team. A lady wanted prayer and as I interviewed her, she told me why she needed prayer. While I prayed for what she wanted, the Holy Spirit as a still small voice inside of me kept impressing me to ask about her boyfriend. In obedience, I asked her about her boyfriend and she was SHOCKED! "How did you know?" she asked. I said that God revealed this to me so she could be set free because He loved her. That night, she was set free when we prayed for her real need.

God works to free His people and the workers are few. That is why this book was written. This book is for you, who are open to the light, want to live victoriously and tell others the good news!

CONTENTS

DEDICATION 2
PREMISE FOR THIS WORK iv
HOW TO USE THESE CHAPTERS vi
INTRODUCTION viii
CHAPTER 1 HUMILITY AND REPENTANCE 1
CHAPTER 2 FORGIVENESS 11
CHAPTER 3 RECONCILIATION 23
CHAPTER 4 SANCTIFICATION: PERSONAL GROWTH PLAN FOR
ASSIMILATION & PRINCIPLE PRACTICE 31
CONCLUSION 36
SUGGESTED READING LIST 37
APPENDIX 40
USING A WAY OF LIFE IN GROUP SETTINGS 41
DEPENDENCE ON GOD 44
DECISION-MAKING / PROBLEM-SOLVING PROCESS 46
MY LIFE PHILOSOPHY 53
MY PRAISE SONG 59
DEAR LITTLE ONE 60
THE SERENITY PRAYER 61
COME, CHILD OF MY LOVE 63
THE GRIEF PROCESS 65
GOAL SETTING 69
BIBLIOGRAPHY 75
ABOUT THE AUTHOR 80

As each part of A Way of Life can be purchased separately, some of the same writings are duplicated in some or each part of this book series. Examples include the growth plan and, in the appendix, goal setting.

xiii

CHAPTER 1

HUMILITY AND REPENTANCE

As you ask God for His will to be done in your life, He will begin to work. He knew you from the beginning, knows what will fulfill you and is waiting for you to invite Him to work with you. What more could you want, for His will is perfect for you! Pray to Him, tell Him of any doubts and look for Him to work.

HUMILITY

According to J. Keith Miller in his book A Hunger for Healing (N.Y.: Harper Collins, 1991), humility is seeing yourself as you are; good and bad, strong and weak and then acting authentically (honestly) on those truths. Without humility, you can't truly change as you are not fully open to being changed. Without humility, you are unable to see yourself honestly and it's a choice. Just remember that you are loved unconditionally and can live in grace e.g., making mistakes but learning and changing from them without shaming or guilting yourself. You can choose to lay your way down and ask the Holy Spirit to show you His way and watch what He starts showing you!

Along with humility and honesty, congruence can happen. Congruence occurs when what is happening on the inside matches what is happening on the outside. As you walk this way, what you may "pretend to be" is let go and you start living the truth of who you truly are. Miller states, "As we let God remove that which we are not (what we are trying to be) and as we hear and try to be in fact what we potentially are, then we'll be more authentic. Living more in tune with the person God made us to be, we become free from the constant war that has gone on inside about what we should be and do in different areas of our lives" (pg. 120).

As you come to see that you are not God and cannot solve your problems alone, you can also begin to see that you cannot solve others' problems for them. Each believer, according to Philippians 2:12, is responsible before God to work out their "own salvation with fear and trembling" which is a healthy desire to not offend God by disobeying Him. As you turn your problems over to God and talk to Him about them, you can also turn the problems of others over to Him and them to solve. Even though it's not your responsibility to carry another's problems, we all are commanded to "bear one another's burdens" (Galatians 6:2). In context, that means you are to stand with other believers, share each other's lives, sometimes help with time or money and pray for one another. The responsibility *for* others stays with them, "for each one shall bear his own load" (Galatians 6:3). If you attempt to take on responsibilities that are not yours, this act of control and manipulation tempts others to remain as a child which is a great disservice to them. The best thing you can do for others is to point them to Jesus. Allow them to do their own growing and encourage and be there for them along the way. That way, no one walks alone.

An example of this includes a vision that I had for someone else. I was praying in my prayer closet and saw the church that I was attending at the time and some of the folks in it. There was one man that stood out and the word that I heard, was guilt. Mind you, this man speaks prophesy and such in the church so that didn't make sense to me, but I knew it was a word from God for him. I told my husband and asked him to go with me when I shared what I heard from God with this gentleman. When we went to see him, he teared up and shared that he didn't feel worthy and was terribly guilt-ridden. Though his mind believed that Jesus came, died and rose again for his salvation, his heart was not allowing that truth to be for him. He wasn't living in grace, which is unmerited favor. God looks with favor on us as we are His children, His creation. This man was holding himself hostage by not living in the truth of who God says He is. He was playing God and condemning himself.

I want to say that from that day forward that man was set free, but I can't. I don't know what he did with the information God had me tell him and I'm not responsible for any choice he made. I am only responsible to give the message though it makes me sad thinking that he didn't accept God's unconditional love for him and might still be guilt-ridden to this day. In summary, God's way for all of us and you, is to be humble, willing and obedient to do what He tells you to do and then, leave the results to Him. You are His, anyway! Don't condemn yourself if you truly are sorry and repentant over a situation. Fail forward and learn from everything. Learn of and walk in His grace, His unmerited favor. Try it! Trust me, you will like it.

Why is humility so important in receiving God's help?

In what way have you seen humility open yourself up to God?

List some examples that show you are practicing humility:

What has God told you that has meant the most to you so far in your healing?

What one thing has God done for you so far through these chapters?

God says in Ezekiel 11:19-20, *"I will give them one heart and I will put a new spirit within them and take the stony heart out of their flesh and give them a heart of flesh."*

In what way has being humble supported the softening of your heart?

REPENTANCE

Repentance is a sincere, sorrowful acknowledgment of any wrongdoing, an acceptance of the responsibility for your erroneous ways and a sincere, complete forsaking of those ways. The real issue is your heart attitude and whether you are *sincerely serious about changing*. You get to decide whether to give the reins to God to orchestrate your healing rather than trying to control or change yourself. You say, "Yes, Lord," and watch Him work.

As you give the reigns to God to orchestrate your healing, you will begin to understand the error of your ways and how it has affected you and others. A godly sorrow will begin to grow as you understand what your part was, in past situations. It's the sincere, godly sorrow that supports being able to fully repent, not just being sorry for what happened or that you got "caught" or "found out."

When you give the reigns to God to heal you, that does not mean He will heal you without any action on your part. Quite the contrary. This action requires repentance, which is taking to Him the error of your ways, asking Him to change you and then looking to see what action He may require you to take to participate in your healing. When you sincerely repent, your attitudes, through the operation of the Holy Spirit, begin to align themselves according to His attitudes which brings release. Other times, He may give you opportunities to practice the opposite of what you want Him to take away from you. For example, if you ask Him to take impatience away, He may begin to give you opportunities to practice patience. He did that with me! See the Dependence of God wheel, found in the appendix.

As you come to Him in repentance, your sensitivity will grow in discerning the opportunities He is placing before you to practice the new skills He is working in you. It is up to you to walk through these opportunities. You will face a variety of temptations but know for sure that "no temptation has overtaken you except such as is common to man; but God is faithful, who will not allow you to be tempted beyond what you are able, but...will also make the way of escape, that you may be able to bear it" (1 Corinthians 10:13). *The way out is through.* As you do this, you will experience a strengthening and understanding of His direction and operation in your life, which will enable you to open up to Him even more. Those around you had better watch out because soon you'll be flying instead of crawling!

Reasons to repent:

- God commands us to
- Lack of honesty to yourself and others fosters ill health physically, mentally, spiritually and relationally
- All works will be shown in the end times anyway
- God knows anyway
- Repentance is required for forgiveness as it shows that you

sincerely want to change

How to repent:

- Sincerely ask God to change your heart attitude/s to align with His ways
- Acknowledge what steps you can take to foster that change (e.g., treating others differently, being aware of self-serving motives and confessing and turning away from them as needed)
- Accept God's forgiveness (not condemn yourself if you have sincerely repented)

You can tell you have truly repented if you are going in a different direction. An example is an army changing course when the general commands the change. It is noticeable immediately if we are sincere.

With the Holy Spirit within you supporting your transformation to be more like Jesus, you will be amazed that an increasing desire grows to be obedient to God's will and way. As you feel, hear and follow the leading of the Holy Spirit, you will experience the blessings that are yours and only yours. You will begin to understand the beauty and benefits of His way as you walk in it. God's will and way is so much more than a matter of dos and don'ts; it is a heart that longs for obedience to God and increasingly is. As we follow God's way, we are freed to be who we were created to be, which is love.

My understanding of repentance is:

What fears do you have when you contemplate repentance?

How have you seen your heart change thus far?

In what areas do you want obedience to occur?

Letting go of things, even in repentance, entails a loss. Being human, you likely will or have grieved when you experienced a loss, which is not a comfortable experience. You may not want to feel your grief and may run from letting go of things in your life; even when you know you will benefit. With any loss, turn to God and ask Him to help you let go and participate with Him in getting rid of what He wants to get rid of, in your life.

(See the Grief Process in the appendix)

What is your fear of feeling your pain?

What do you fear will happen if you let go of something that you have been holding onto?

List the people, situations and sins (wrongdoings) you are still holding onto and the reason you are holding onto them.

People/Situations/Wrongdoings	Reason
1.	
2.	
3.	
4.	
5.	
6.	
7.	
8.	
9.	
10.	
11.	
12.	
13.	
14.	
15.	

CHAPTER 2

FORGIVENESS

FORGIVENESS

If you hold bitterness or resentment towards others and condemn them, who do you think is paying for this? If you hold this bitterness inside, how does it feel? Do you want to live with yourself with resentment, bitterness and yucky feelings inside? Do you want to walk through your life this way? Do you want to be like those you condemn? If you said no to those questions, good for you! Unforgiveness is like keeping a garbage bag on your back filled with all the hurt you have received, which only serves to weigh you down and keep you in pain. Unforgiveness only hurts you and can support you being like those you don't like. Additionally, the other individuals involved in any of your situations likely don't remember what you did or what they did to you. You remember because what they did hurt you. Please know that forgiveness doesn't make light of what you've been through. However, holding onto hurt only serves to keep you from having healthy and whole relationships. God says, "Forgive and you will be forgiven." This scripture tells you to forgive first and you will then be forgiven which is hard for many individuals. The good news is that it's possible.

You get to do what you can to repair the broken and bruised relationships of the past as you can't move forward to the present and future unless you do. You get to address the relationships that have caused guilt, shame, pain and resentment, as they continue to distance you from God, others and yourself. Give *ALL* your emotions in prayer to God and watch what happens within you! It's a miracle of release and freedom. However, if you do not release your negative pent-up emotions from all the guilt and pain in your life, these feelings will skew a realistic viewing and evaluation of all your relationships. Worse yet, you'll keep making the same choices to put yourself into the same types of situations, if you don't change.

Now this does not mean that you are to keep harmful relationships in your life. Evaluating relationships is to identify the harm you have done to others, to yourself and what others have done to you. It is taking responsibility for your actions, confessing the same, asking for forgiveness and asking how you are to act, next time. It is forgiving others and yourself and letting go of all the negative pent-up energy and emotions that are destroying you. This is a preparatory step to moving out and loving others and yourself (the beginning of reconciliation). This chapter also asks if you are willing to make amends to *ALL*.

As you apply these kingdom principles for living victoriously, the Holy Spirit can support you as you begin training to catch yourself when you justify or explain away your behavior. Ask Him to show you your behavior and watch what will happen. It is His will to show you, so He will do so and if your behavior is wrong, don't justify it. Just admit it and when you acknowledge it as such, distortion and denial of the truth fall away. When you admit wrongdoing right away, you won't have to ask for forgiveness later and relationships work much better! When there are conflicts, acknowledging the wrong, your sorrow for the wrong and your responsibility quickly, will usually open the door to why the scenario went as it did. That is how looking with understanding begins between individuals and prevents more hurt from happening to or through you. Catching yourself early will stop many communications from going sour.

A Way Of Life

To support this process, we will discuss a tool to easily do this in a later chapter. However, before we move on from this topic, it is important to address forgiving yourself. Have you done that? Or do you keep yourself on the hook and keep condemning yourself (guilt and shame) for past and present actions or decisions? If you have accepted Jesus' death and resurrection for your sins (past, present and future) then God has forgiven you and sees you flawless. God sees you as white as snow and unblemished as Jesus' blood covers ALL your sins. He paid for them with his blood on the cross and hence, God sees you with unmerited favor (grace). This grace is *extremely* important in your walk with Christ and sadly, not apprehended and lived out by many Christians. You can fail forward, meaning that you make mistakes, yet learn from them while forgiving yourself. With what you learn, you change on the inside so that the *same mistakes* don't constantly keep happening throughout your life. Living and learning without false guilt is heaven on earth!

Along with grace, you also won't get the punishment you deserve (mercy) as you learn, change and forgive yourself. Isn't this good news? You can let yourself off the hook! No more false guilt and shame and you can have joy in being forgiven and free. The question is, will you let yourself off the hook and be free? I encourage you to begin a new day and choose today to let yourself be free. Trust God to give individuals their due and walk daily in forgiveness towards yourself and others and begin to walk in freedom from negative emotions and lies. As God says, "...the truth shall make you free," John 8:23.

Scripture to memorize: Luke 6:37,
"Forgive, and you will be forgiven."

To help identify relationships that have hurt you, make a list of the people you get to forgive and the offense involved.

Person	Offense
1.	
2.	
3.	
4.	
5.	
6.	
7.	
8.	
9.	
10.	
11.	
12.	
13.	
14.	
15.	

Scripture to memorize this week: Matthew 7:7, "Ask, and it will be given to you; seek, and you will find; knock, and it will be opened to you."

Many times, you may not realize how you are hurting others or how they are hurting you. Here are helpful guidelines for identifying harmful situations and knowing what to do.

- Someone is accusing you of doing something hurtful. Instead of being defensive, listen carefully and maybe take notes. Evaluate the criticism. Don't justify the behavior.

- Are you telling others what to do and giving your opinion even when it is not desired? That can be a form of controlling because, as Christians, we may think we are being helpful and know what is right. Especially if our opinion is not asked for.

- Be sensitive to communication as it ebbs and flows. What stopped the flow? Did you say something that might have harmed the other and shut down the communication process? Stop right away and ask. It is better to clarify than to walk away not knowing what happened. If you walk away without the error/s being addressed, the next time you meet the individual there may be residual reservations about entering a conversation since the previous conversation had no resolution or was uncomfortable.

- Are you blaming others or using silent treatment? Blaming destroys others and you. No one prospers under the silent treatment or blame so let go of both and open the conversation. Begin talking!

As you move along these chapters, you hopefully have begun to see that the values that society promotes—status, control, excitement and fun, are not the important things in life. Rather, as the truth flourishes and the Holy Spirit awakens within you, perhaps you see that the important things in life are loving, intimate and healthy relationships. Especially an open, intimate relationship with God, our Father. This, in turn, will give you more serenity and the ability to really enjoy living. You can stop running, sink your roots down, be yourself, and have loads of fun!

What harmful behaviors do you see yourself doing in relationships (e.g., gossiping, or being domineering, sarcastic, aggressive, or passive)?

Why do you think you operate this way?

A Way Of Life

What does God say is your responsibility toward others, in Romans 3:10, "Love does no harm to a neighbor?"

How can you become more sensitive to when harm is being done in a relationship?

Give an example where you noticed relational harm being done and you took steps right away to rectify the harm:

How would any unforgiveness on your part serve to block your progress and hurt your relationship with God? Matthew 6:14-15 says, "If you forgive men their trespasses, your heavenly Father will also forgive you. But if you do not forgive men their trespasses, neither will your Father forgive your trespasses."

God says, in Romans 12:19, "Do not avenge yourselves, but rather give place to wrath (put anger and vengeance away); for it is written, 'Vengeance is Mine; I will repay,' says the Lord."

What does God say about His responsibility towards those who harmed or hurt you?

What feelings come up in you at the command that it is not your place to get even with others—that it is God's place?

Do you believe that others will get their due?

What reluctance do you have to let God give others their due?

Many times, you will not see others get their due. You may be out of their lives when their due comes to them, but you can rest assured that anyone who does not commit their lives to God's way will pay; either in this life or eternity.

Making amends means attempting to heal the relationship through communication or actions, such as restitution (giving back more than what was stolen and attempting to make things better than they were).

How will letting go of unforgiveness and making amends set you free?

What do you hope to gain by making amends?

What do you fear most in making amends?

The following prayer will support you as you decide to release others and/or yourself from the slavery of pent-up negative emotions such as blame, guilt and shame, to name a few. Say the following out loud and fill in the blanks with whom you are releasing (even yourself) from the jailhouse of your resentment. Let yourself and others off the hook.

A PRAYER FOR RELEASE FROM RESENTMENT

By Peter Marshall, Congressional Chaplin

Lord Jesus, You know me through and through. You know that I have steadily refused to forgive (insert name) who has wronged me, yet I have had the audacity often to seek Your forgiveness for my own wrongdoing.

The acids of bitterness and a vengeful spirit have threatened to eat away my peace. Yet I have stubbornly rationalized every unlovely motive. I have said, "I am clearly in the right. It is only human to dislike a few people. (Insert name) deserves no forgiveness." How well I know that neither have I ever deserved forgiveness, which You have always freely granted me.

So, Lord Jesus, I ask You now for the grace to forgive this hurt. Even now, I am divided about it, only partially willing to release it. But you can manage even my reluctance, my loitering feet. Take now my divided will and make it of one piece, wholly Your will.

And Lord, I give to You this emotion of resentment, which clings as if glued to my heart. Wrest (take) it from me. Cleanse every petty thought. Make me sweet again. I dare to ask that You will not only forgive me to the extent that I have forgiven (insert name/s), but that You will bless (insert name/s) to the degree that You have blessed me.

For these great mercies I thank You, in Your name, who gave me the supreme example in forgiving even those who slew You (on the cross). Amen.

Peter Marshall—Chaplain of the U.S. Senate from 1947-1949. Cited in The Prayers of Peter Marshall by Catherine Marshall (N.Y.: Inspirational Press ed., 1996), p. 324. Updated Thee and Thy usage.

CHAPTER 3

RECONCILIATION

RECONCILIATION

In one sense, God's whole message centers around this principle as He is the one who sent Jesus to die on the cross for our sins to reconcile us to Him. He gave us the example of being the initiator of the reconciliation process. God opened the door to Himself by sending His Son, Jesus, to die so that you may enter a covenant relationship with Him. In other words, God sent Jesus to reconcile you, through Jesus' death and resurrection, with Himself and through Jesus, there is no barrier to unity and peace with our Maker, God. Reconciliation results in peace where once there was enmity (division, hatred, animosity). Therefore, if you do not incorporate this principle in your life, God's peace will not be yours.

Reconciliation with others also denotes leaving no impediment to unity and peace. Hence, no bitterness, evil thoughts, unforgiveness, or anything hindering peace is to remain between individuals. You, a child of the Most High God, are called to be a peacemaker and treat others as you would want to be treated. Being a peacemaker requires responsibility on your part to try to repair broken or wounded relationships, even if you are not the one who did the wrong. You are called to reach out to bring unity and harmony in every relationship even if you are the first to reach out. You are responsible before God for your actions, not another's. Therefore, the following deals with you and your responsibility in the reconciliation process.

Cultivating sensitivity in your relationship with God and others empowers you to be aware when friction is present in a relationship. An ounce of preventive maintenance is much better than a pound of cure, so address this friction right away so it does not fester or worsen, and reconciliation then becomes necessary.

Reconciliation takes place through confession, understanding and forgiveness. With any wrongdoings, take any actions, emotions, motives and thoughts to God and ask Him to show you where these feelings, thoughts and actions are coming from, the root cause. Whatever you find, ask God for forgiveness while being direct and honest, stating what wrong has been done and when you can, confess the wrong to the other individual. Take responsibility for your behavior and the wrong attitude or motives that prompted it, expressing remorse. Ask God to create a clean heart and spirit within you. All this takes courage when living to do the right thing for yourself and others. It's not easy but it's worth it.

Look to reconcile your relationship with God first and your mind, spirit and heart will be clearer as you attempt to be a peacemaker with others and confess your wrong to another. Training yourself to be a peacemaker and confessing and repenting of the heart attitudes that are keeping you from acting in God's ways are key to having harmonious relationships with God and others.

In approaching someone to make amends or reconcile with them, do know that there is a risk with taking this action. You won't know whether you will be rejected or accepted for your efforts, especially when you try to make amends with your enemies. Still, you are called to make amends to all and if fear arises within you, walk through it and make amends anyway. Don't let fear stop you and as you learn God's Kingdom Principles for Living Victoriously, you will learn that fear is of the devil and most times, isn't real (fear = false evidence appearing real).

In attempting reconciliation, it is best to meet face-to-face whenever possible. Much is stated in non-verbal communication, and you can better perceive whether amends are happening or not. If the person you want to make amends with has passed away, some individuals have found it helpful to write a letter telling the person what you would have said in person. It is in the confession of the spoken, written, or signed word that healing happens.

What are you to do if a person refuses to participate in the reconciliation process? For reconciliation to occur between two people, it does take two. If another does not accept your attempt to reconcile the relationship, the next step would be to confess your part in the disparity of the relationship to God and accept His pardon. You may also feel it is necessary to confess your part to a close friend but first examine your motives before deciding to do this. Do you want to gossip about so and so who does not want to reconcile the relationship, or do you sincerely want to confess a wrong you did? Do you feel genuine sorrow and concern for the damaged relationship?

Once you have done the above and dealt with your part in any relational friction, you are free in the reconciliatory process. If the other individual does not accept your attempt/s, that person is guilty before God for not being willing to make amends and have peace in the relationship. Therefore, wait patiently, hoping and looking always for a change towards reconciliation. You are not instructed to keep going to the other person to try to fix the relationship only to get rebuffed time and time again, unless the Holy Spirit is prompting you to do so. You can let another be and let God work within them and trust that He will, though you may not see the result.

Apologies differ from reconciliation. You can apologize for doing something wrong, but unless your behavior changes (recall Chapter 1—repentance), reconciliation cannot happen as this sorrow is not heartfelt. Many individuals say they are sorry but are only sorry because they got caught; not sorry about what they did. They also don't plan on acting differently in the future and you will be able to tell if someone or you is truly sorrowful or just acting. Acting sorry is not true repentance and reconciliation is not true from that person or from you if you are just acting. Make sure to evaluate yourself to ensure that you are not acting that way!

What about when someone has done something wrong to you and comes to you first to make amends and reconcile the relationship? How do you react? In acceptance or in anger? Remember to take all feelings to God and allow Him to work His truth in you and if necessary, ask for a cooling period if the relationship is volatile. If you take a cooling period, make sure you return to this relationship to make amends and bring reconciliation as we are called to be at peace with all.

The biggest obstacle to making amends is pride. You may not want others to think less or differently towards you, so you hesitate. The good news, though, is when you look to reconcile, the opposite usually happens. By your actions, people know you care about them, about yourself and they respect you and appreciate your efforts. Pride binds but humility frees. Which do you choose?

Scripture to memorize: Matthew 5:9, "Blessed are the peacemakers, for they shall be called sons of God."

How has seeking revenge hurt you in the past?

Feelings surface when we risk being honest with others about our feelings and faults. List those that come up for you:

Give an example where you apologized but as it was not heartfelt sorrow, reconciliation didn't happen:

What feelings do you have when you consider reconciling with someone who has hurt you or who you have hurt?

List an example and the result of a reconciliation that you have had with someone you know:

List an example and the result of a reconciliation that you participated in during the past two weeks:

What were your feelings after you reconciled and made amends?

Sometimes situations will not require going to an individual for reconciliation to occur. You will know if this is the case and you can go directly to God, ask for forgiveness, and move on. You don't want to avoid your responsibility, so a close evaluation gets to occur in deciding whether you are to go to that person. Perhaps more harm than good may occur? Wisdom is needed and seeking counsel may be in order if you wonder if you are to make amends in a certain situation.

Make a list of amends you want to make. Is there anything on your list of amends that may cause more harm than good?

If so, which one and why?

When seeking reconciliation, it is necessary to pray for sensitivity in timing. In one situation, you may be able to make amends right away. In another, waiting for the right timing is best. Example: If your emotions are still too close to the surface, you may not be able to make a clean amend. A clean amend or reconciliation means that the attempt at reconciliation is not tainted by anything other than wanting the relationship repaired. Evaluating, confessing, and repenting of your motives, heart attitudes, and emotions before you act is imperative on your part to make a clean reconciliation attempt to repair any relationship. If our heart's attitude is one of care and love with the desire that the relationship be repaired, we will be free from the responsibility of a negative outcome. We can only do our part.

CHAPTER 4

SANCTIFICATION: PERSONAL GROWTH PLAN FOR ASSIMILATION & PRINCIPLE PRACTICE

Sanctification, according to Merriam-Webster, is defined as "the state of growing in divine grace as a result of Christian commitment after baptism or conversion." It is growing in grace and our emphasis is on the word, growing. This is not a stagnant walk, nor is it boring! But it is worth it. ☺ This principle was covered in depth in Book 2 but is covered again to look at applying the principles just reviewed.

I call a certain time in my life, baptism by fire. I was living in a marriage with my unfaithful husband and believed that God could change my marriage (which I do believe is the truth if BOTH parties are willing). So, I stayed in the marriage, hoping my husband would change his heart and mind. I knew that I was responsible for my part in the marriage, so began to pray that God would show me whatever I was doing wrong and change me. I asked God to create a clean heart in me and change my heart attitudes, motives and behaviors.

I went to God daily and asked Him to have His Holy Spirit search me. He began to show me gently what needed to be changed and as a gentleman, heal and clean my heart and teach me His ways. As I read the bible, I began to see how relationships and God's universal principles work and I became thankful for what He was showing me.

Look in the Appendix at the Dependence on God wheel. These are the sanctification steps and the first one is being willing. Therefore, be sincere and willing to become aware of what doesn't line up with God's ways through reading His word. Ask Him to change what He shows you, on the inside, and do not resist the change. You'll be changing from the inside out (instead of trying to "put the change on") and the change will stick. Do whatever action He says to do and don't worry or be scared, even if what you are learning is painful to admit or you don't completely understand, yet. God is a gentleman and He will only collaborate with you to the point that you allow Him to. Do you want to be fully healed? Free from all your fears? Don't resist and seek the Lord. He will be with you 100% of the way. As you don't resist, you will gain as the following depicts:

"No pain, No gain."

These are the words the athletes sing
As they work their muscles to the sting.

"It hurts, it hurts," they cry
As the burning goes deeper and deeper into their thigh.

And yet they push on to never-ending fights,
Knowing that without this pain, they would never reach the heights.

And so, I say to you — you who so resist your pain —
Work it to the bone and do not deter,
For with your pain, you will gain.

—WHAT WE RESIST, PERSISTS—

PLAN

The intent of this book is the understanding and application of the information and principles covered, which is imperative for living victoriously. Below is a growth and development plan for you to utilize to solidify these life-giving principles in your life and all the lives that this work touches.

To create a personal growth development plan, start by defining what you've learned and what you want your results to be. Make sure you write them down. Next, perform a self-assessment and identify one area that needs attention. Then, determine the required actions and develop an action plan using the "SMARTER" goal-setting method, found in the appendix.

Here is an example of a growth plan.

What I want: To be effective as a family and work leader.

What I do now:	What I learned:	What I will change:	The time period to practice my change:	The outcome:
I tend to control others and situations. I don't listen and make collaborative decisions with others.	I learned that surrendering frees me to be me. and that I don't have control over others. I only can control myself.	Listen with my heart before I speak. Listen for the truth and work with it only.	By the end of the next month.	1. My coworkers and family will notice and say something. 2. I will feel open on the inside rather than stressed and closed off.

Implement with goals: (see appendix on how to set goals)

Examples of SMARTER goals with its supporting activities to reach the stated goal:

Goal: By the end of next month, my family and coworker will see me as an effective leader as evidenced by them saying something about my behavior change and I will have a stress score reduction from an 8 to a 4 by the end of next month.

Specific:	Yes (simple and clear)
Measurable:	stress score lower, family & coworkers will say something about my behavior change
Achievable:	this is achievable
Realistic:	this is realistic
Timely:	end of the next month
Evaluate goal:	end of next month and stress level reduction level
Reset goal:	change it, extend the end time, or create another goal

Activities:

1. For the next month, at work and in every meeting, I will not be the first to speak and share my opinion. I will share...just not first!

2. For the next month, I will listen with my heart to what my family says and seek to understand their perspective before stating mine. I will do that by asking questions.

Now, it's your turn!

On a separate piece of paper that you can hang where you will see it frequently, type or write out your growth plan to assimilate and apply the principles you just learned. Find a safe friend who will listen and share your plan with them and as someone I know says, "git'r done!"

CONCLUSION

As A Way of Life, in its full workbook format, was so meaty, I was advised to divide the work into multiple small courses. Therefore, I have divided A Way of Life, Kingdom Principles for Living Victoriously, into 4 parts and this concludes Book 3. There is much more that leads to peace within and I want to encourage you to continue learning and applying God's principles so that you *will* experience freedom and peace within.

To continue your journey, in your internet browser, type in AWayofLifeMinistries.com. Click on the Bookstore or Courses tab to find resources and purchase whatever you need to continue your journey and growth. You can also search on Amazon for A Way of Life by Nancy Williams to purchase from there.

Please let us know how your journey is going by using the Contact Us form on the website to connect with us. We would LOVE to hear from you about how you are progressing. You can also subscribe to our blog page and we'll keep you informed of upcoming events, new publications, online courses and book offerings. Hope to hear from you soon and if you have questions, please ask!

Blessings on your journey

~ Nancy ~

SUGGESTED READING LIST

The following 4 books are secular but may be helpful. Read them with caution and a biblically discerning mind.

- Beattie, Melody. (1987). Codependent No More. New York: Harper & Row.
- Bradshaw, John. (1988). The Family. Florida: Health Communications, Inc.
- Fromm, Erich. (1956). The Art of Loving. New York: Harper & Row.
- Peck, M. Scott, MD. (1978). The Road Less Traveled. New York: Simon & Schuster, Inc.

The following list is from a Christian perspective. I encourage you to read especially Francis Schaeffer's, True Spirituality, R.A. Torry's, The Person and Work of the Holy Spirit and J. Keith Miller's, A Hunger for Healing.

- Bennett, Dennis and Rita. (1971). The Holy Spirit and You. New Jersey: Logos International.
- Bridges, Jerry. (1978). The Pursuit of Holiness. Colorado: Navpress.
- Bridges, Jerry. (1983). The Practice of Godliness. Colorado: Navpress.
- Buhler, Rich. (1988). Pain and Pretending. Tennessee: Thomas Nelson, Inc.
- Esses, Michael. (1974). The Phenomenon of Obedience. New

Jersey: Logos International.

- Huggett, Joyce. (1986). The Joy of Listening to God. Illinois: InterVarsity Press.
- Miller, J. Keith. (1991). A Hunger for Healing. New York: Harper Collins.
- Powell, John. (1969). Why Am I Afraid to Tell You Who I Am?. Illinois: Argus Communications.
- Powell, John. (1974). The Secret of Staying in Love. Texas: Argus Communications.
- Powell, John. (1976). Fully Human, Fully Alive. Illinois: Argus Communications.
- Powell, John. (1978). Unconditional Love. Texas: Argus Communications.
- Schaeffer, Francis A. (1971). True Spirituality. Illinois: Tyndale House Publishers.
- Seamands, David A. (1981). Healing for Damaged Emotions. Illinois: SP Publications, Inc.
- Smalley, Gary and Trent, John, Ph.D. (1986), The Blessing. Tennessee: Thomas Nelson, Inc.
- Smith, Chuck. (1979,1980). Effective Prayer Life. California: The Word For Today.
- Swindoll, Charles R. (1983). Dropping Your Guard. New York: Bantam Books.
- Torrey, R.A. (1974). The Person & Work of the Holy Spirit (rev. ed.). Michigan: Zondervan Publishing House.
- Watson, David. (1980). The Hidden Battle. Illinois: Harold Shaw Publishers.

- Whitfield, Charles L., M.D. (1987). Healing the Child Within. Florida: Health Communications, Inc.

- Wilkerson, David; and Sherrill, John & Elizabeth. (1963). The Cross and The Switchblade. New Jersey: Spire Books.

APPENDIX

It is recommended to review and use all the resources in this appendix to continue your growth journey and find your blessings as you do so.

USING *A WAY OF LIFE IN GROUP SETTINGS*..41
DEPENDENCE ON GOD...44
DECISION-MAKING / PROBLEM-SOLVING PROCESS.........................46
MY LIFE PHILOSOPHY..53
MY PRAISE SONG..59
DEAR LITTLE ONE...60
THE SERENITY PRAYER..61
COME, CHILD OF MY LOVE..63
THE GRIEF PROCESS..65
GOAL SETTING...69
BIBLIOGRAPHY...75
ABOUT THE AUTHOR...80

USING A WAY OF LIFE IN GROUP SETTINGS

This book has been used in multiple group settings, so the below has been included to support group success and encourage individuals to be facilitators. Usually, there is sharing of what God is doing in each person and what spoke to them from the chapter being reviewed.

GROUP LEADERS

Ground Rules, which are to be read to the small group:

- Confidentiality is of utmost importance
- Please don't put down another's person, thoughts, or opinions—each person is of equal value
- It's OK to say that you don't want to share
- Please share time equally. Give everyone a chance to share
- One person talks at a time
- Please be personal. Use "I" or "me" statements
- We work together as a team
- Talk from feelings, not stories or circumstances
- Don't give advice
- Listen and try to understand what is being said

Good Family Functional Rules taken from Bradshaw on: The Family by John Bradshaw. Copyright 1988. Health Communications, Inc. Used with permission from the author and if used in the group, the group will be healthy. Facilitators are to read the following Functional Rules at the beginning of each group..

- Problems are acknowledged and resolved
- 5 freedoms—can be expressed and explored with no judgment:
    - perceptions
    - feelings
    - thoughts
    - desires
    - fantasies
- Communication is direct, specific and behavioral
- Family members get their needs met
- Family members can be different
- Parents do what they say (self-disciplined disciplinarians)
- Atmosphere is fun and spontaneous
- The rules require accountability
- Violation of another's values leads to guilt
- Mistakes are forgiven and viewed as learning tools
- Individuals are in touch with their healthy shame
- The family systems exist for each other

What to discuss in the group setting:

- What was particularly meaningful to you from the last chapter?
- How do you see this affecting your life right now?
- Are there any changes that you want to make?

Closing in Prayer: What can we pray about tonight or during this coming week?

DEPENDENCE ON GOD

See below, where God is in the middle and all the spokes have their focus on Him and His way. Walk through steps 1-11 in order and watch the results within yourself! The result is having the change desired.

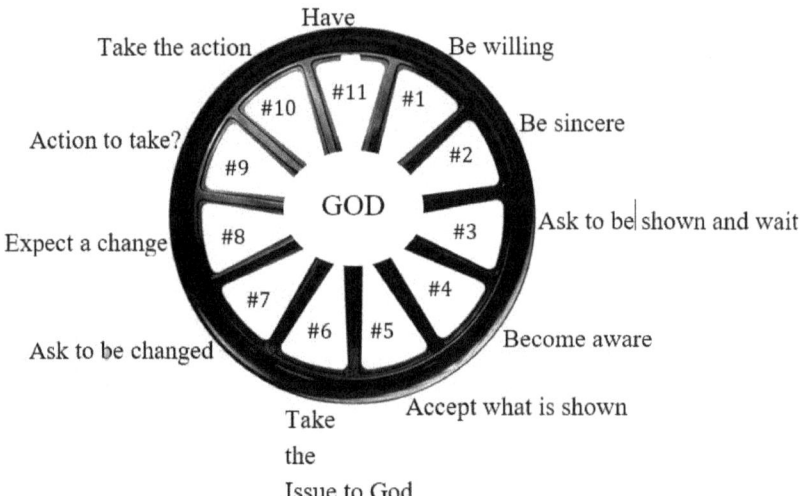

The beginning of your dependence on God starts with your being willing and goes until you BE, DO and then Have, regarding each situation. Be willing & sincere, ask to be shown and God will open your heart and you will begin to be aware of what you get to know. Accepting this knowledge is critical to your personal & spiritual growth. Take what God shows you back to Him and ask for it and for you to be changed. Expect Him to work within you and you will know when things are changing. He may show you some action to take, so make sure you complete the action and you will be closer to being or having what He wants you to be or have.

This cycle works for everything and while most elements are important, being willing and sincere to ask to be shown what needs to be changed, or ask for understanding, etc. is most important. If you are not sincere or willing, this cycle of growth and understanding will not work.

Point # 1	You are WILLING
Point # 2	You are SINCERE
Point # 3	You ASK TO BE SHOWN
Point # 4	You are AWARE
Point # 5	You ACCEPT WHAT WE ARE SHOWN
Point # 6	You TAKE THE ISSUE TO GOD
Point # 7	You ASK TO BE CHANGED
Point # 8	You EXPECT A CHANGE
Point # 9	You look for what ACTION TO TAKE
Point # 10	You TAKE THE ACTION
Point # 11	You BE, DO, then HAVE

To refresh the understanding of what is meant by the BE—DO—HAVE statement, refer to the introduction at the beginning of this book. Then, enjoy and experience the newfound freedom which God gives to you as you submit and depend on Him!

DECISION-MAKING / PROBLEM-SOLVING PROCESS

Below are the steps to support the making of informed decisions. Looking at the consequences of each of the choices to make when making decisions prepares you to commit or not commit to that decision. While you may not always know future consequences, seeking wise counsel is a great tool to use to assist you in making decisions, regardless of the decision size.

Step 1

Determine the problem or decision facing you.

Step 2

Determine what is causing the problem.

Step 3

Consider your options from a biblical perspective. What alternative actions can you take?

Step 4

Determine the consequences of each of the options before you.

Step 5

Pray for wisdom and boldness in doing the will of God, seek godly counsel for important matters and decide based on all the information you have available to you at the time.

Step 6

> Act on your decision.

Step 7

> Evaluate your decision.

Step 8

> Modify the decision as needed. Rejoice if things work out well but if they don't, you need not regard your decision as a failure. Just learn from it, which is failing forward! Take responsibility for your own choices and do not blame others if what you desired does not occur or something terrible happened. Make the Serenity Prayer your own when making tough decisions: "God, grant me the serenity to accept the things I cannot change, the courage to change the things I can and the wisdom to know the difference."

TIME TO PRACTICE!

Now that you have the steps, it is time to practice!

What is the problem?

What is causing the problem?

What alternative actions can you take?

Option 1:

Option 2:

Option 3:

What consequences will happen with each of the above options?

Option 1--consequences:

Option 2--consequences:

Option 3--consequences:

Most of us have been taught to think in black and white, with usually only one right decision to make. We often fail to look at ALL the factors inherent in a situation before deciding on a course of action. Many times, we just react. Exploring all the avenues of action God gives us for addressing decisions and problems will keep us from unnecessarily boxing ourselves in. It frees us to work cooperatively and collaboratively with others.

The course of action you have decided on is:

After the action was completed, the result was:

I need to change my decision in the following way:

I have learned the following about the decision-making process:

MY LIFE PHILOSOPHY

(WHY YOU DO WHAT YOU DO)

After this section is information on Goal Setting. Before setting goals, you first get to dig deep and discover your life philosophy because goal setting is not effective unless it's something that causes your heart to sing. Your life's philosophy is that which guides your actions, decisions, goals and how you live your life. It stems from the fundamental beliefs that you hold which direct and guide you daily. It might even make you cry! To identify why you do what you do, examining your life and what beliefs you hold now is where you want to start.

Socrates said, "The unexamined life is not worth living." That is so true! How can you move forward if you don't live, examine yourself, your decisions, your path in life and learn? No more. It's time to dig deep.

You have a philosophy of life whether you think you do or not. It can be seen in how you spend your time and money, what you view as important, how you see and treat others and what is in your heart that might make you cry. All too often, you don't do what you view or say is important and don't accomplish what you want to with your life because you have not reflected on these important things and weren't taught how to do this. Because of this, you may have taken on what society or others view as important and life flies by, not being truly lived according to the destiny ordained for you by your Creator. PLEASE STOP and don't let this continue if your life is flying by and being lived without purpose! You were created for a purpose and are a valuable, cherished individual. So, let's look at what's important to you and write out *your* life philosophy.

The following are elements that you get to evaluate prior to writing your life philosophy. Don't worry! An example is included to show how to write what's important to you.

ELEMENTS:

1. My values are: (the bottom line of a philosophy)
2. My beliefs about the world, life, other people and the universe are:
3. What I want to accomplish or live out:
4. How I intend to accomplish the above:

In the spaces provided below, write what you believe to be true today under each category.

1. MY VALUES:

2. MY BELIEFS ABOUT THE WORLD, LIFE, OTHER PEOPLE AND THE UNIVERSE:

3. WHAT I WANT TO ACCOMPLISH OR LIVE OUT:

4. HOW I INTEND TO ACCOMPLISH THE ABOVE:

LIFE PHILOSOPHY EXAMPLE

I believe that God created all things. I believe that Jesus won the battle over Satan when He died on the cross and rose from the dead with the resultant breaking of the bondage to sin for those who believe.

Because of this belief, I will live my life under God's protection and provision and live as His Spirit teaches me; in power, freedom and joy as His child—a child of the King and called to excellence as his ambassador, not perfection. Only He is perfect.

I want my life to show:

- That I care for people above all else
- Joy, peace and freedom
- Depth of character

I will accomplish what I want my life to show by:

- Accepting the responsibility for my choices and life and that what happens or doesn't happen, is up to me (I will live by choice and responsibility and will not play the blame game)
- Training myself to stop and actively listen when others speak (I will be humble and loving)
- Staying repentant and having an attitude of not my will, but Yours be done (I will stay submitted to almighty God)
- Accept beneficial as well as adverse circumstances, knowing that what touches me is only what has been allowed by my Creator and Father (I will walk in surrender and acceptance and foster gratefulness)
- Seeking to learn from the error of my ways (I will be humble and fail forward by learning from my mistakes)

- Enjoying and rejoicing in what God originally gave us to rule and subdue (Genesis 1:28 and fighting in the front lines in my spiritual armor [Ephesians 6:10-19] against the enemy of our souls)

- Studying and obeying God's Word first and foremost (I will seek truth)

Use this page to write out your own life philosophy. Eloquence is not necessary as this is only for you. Review it occasionally and revise as needed.

My Life Philosophy: Date

MY PRAISE SONG

My pain is real. It hurts. At times, I feel as if I am dead inside. Other times I feel as if my heart is breaking into pieces. But—I have come to appreciate my pain for what it teaches me.

I feel solid inside when I acknowledge my pain, which is a special feeling for me. Far too often in the past, I have been tossed to and fro, not wanting to feel my sorrow. I cheated myself of feeling the depth to which my pain goes.

BUT NO MORE

I grow as I experience and listen to my pain. Movement happens within me without my even trying to make it happen. My path becomes clearer before me as I walk with my pain rather than around it.

BUT THERE IS MORE

I have learned that without knowing my pain and sorrow, I cannot fully appreciate and experience the joy that is within me. I have also come to see that as I acknowledge all that is within me, I am experiencing life and living the woman GOD made me to be. When I die, I will know that I have lived life to the fullest: That I have loved well, cried well and have lived fully human, fully alive.

THIS IS MY PRAISE SONG.

I want to acknowledge John Powell's book, Fully Human, Fully Alive, for impacting and inspiring me at a young age.

DEAR LITTLE ONE

Dear little one,

I made you. I love you. Yet you struggle so hard. All around you are voices and messages that say you are no good. I tell you this: They are lying. Do not believe them. When I knit you together in your mother's womb, I used the pattern that was just for you. I used it for no one else. Continue fighting. You must believe what I tell you. I will never lie to you.

You are the person you are supposed to be. You do not have to try to be someone else to be loved by Me. Others may try to tell you that you do. Remember: Do not believe them! You can only be who I made you to be. You cannot be anyone else. It is all I ask of you regarding this. But I do ask you not to be less than I have made you. Be true to yourself and in so doing you will be true to Me. You will please Me.

I love you. I know it is hard and your pain is great. I understand that. But know that the pain will be greater if you try to change who I made you to be, not less.

My child, listen to those whose words and acts prove they love you. Do not believe others. But most of all, listen to Me. For I love you beyond all others. I love you the way I made you. Be that person and love yourself in My Name.

Anonymous

THE SERENITY PRAYER

The serenity prayer is included here, as it points towards dependence upon God, which is what He wants from us. There are great benefits to memorizing this, as God's Holy Spirit will bring it to your remembrance when you need it the most!

God, grant me the serenity to accept the things I cannot change, the courage to change the things that I can and the wisdom to know the difference.

God, grant me the serenity to accept the things I cannot change.

List of things I cannot change:

God, grant me the courage to change the things that I can.

List of things I can change:

God, grant me the wisdom to know the difference.

How I can tell the difference between the two:

COME, CHILD OF MY LOVE

Come and rest in me. Rest, knowing you are My beloved, the apple of My eye. I am right by your side. Never have I been closer, never have I loved you more.

Remember, all that I do, I do in deep abiding love. I am a wise husbandman, seeing the end from the beginning and have purposes of untold love for you and your loved ones.

I called you and chose you from your mother's womb. I have a special plan for your life. You are a chosen vessel of honor; I have set you apart for My special purposes.

Do your nerves wince from a heavy blow that has come upon you? Do not fear: It is shaping you, producing radiance from a precious jewel. I am teaching you the patience of faith, the courage of faith and the victory of faith. Know for sure, precious one, that I am working on your behalf and on behalf of each of your loved ones.

Do you feel crushed under a heavy load? Do you feel you've been broken and lay in useless pieces? Then rejoice and remember it is the broken clay I dwell in most richly. When you are at the end of your strength and wisdom, then I am free to work mightily on your behalf. If you are broken, do not despair: I will use you for My glory. Joseph was broken in Egypt's prison and was prepared for a crown. Moses was broken in the wilderness and led My people free from Egypt's bondage! It is the broken one I use most.

Let patience have her perfect work in this hard place. Your times are in My hand. Do not steal tomorrow out of My hands. Learn to wait on Me. Do not let delays dishearten you, for I am bringing about My perfect will in all of this. In quietness and rest is your strength.

Remember, My ways are perfect. You have given Me your life as a sacred trust and I have received it as such.

Commit your way to Me and I will bring it to pass. No work or plan of Mine can be hindered. You have sought My Kingdom and My will and that you shall have. No matter how things appear, know that I am working all things to the good of those who love Me! I shall have the glory!

Come, I will carry you. Rest in My arms. Do not faint in the day of adversity, for I am your refuge and strength in desperate hours. I will never fail you and you will not fail Me.

Come, rest in my arms. Lay your head upon My breast, trusting in My love and wisdom. I have held nothing back of My love. Since I offered up My precious Son, Jesus, how much more will I help you now? Wait, hope, trust and believe in Me, Child of My love!

Anonymous

THE GRIEF PROCESS

How do you respond to the loss of a dearly loved person or object? The difficulty in overcoming the effects of grief depends on the nature and depth of the loss, your support systems and your ability to feel your sorrow.

To feel grief after a significant loss is normal, natural and to be expected. When you experience loss, you grieve, even if you deny that the grief is there. You can also grieve for what you did not have, such as growing up without your father or mother. You may begin to realize how much you missed their not being around for you.

Grief process—as defined by Dr. Elisabeth Kübler-Ross. (1960). On Death & Dying. Simon & Schuster-Touchstone. Dr. Ross did extensive research on grieving families.

1. Denial
    a. No, I don't want to believe it. It can't be!
    b. Numbness and shock
2. Anger
    a. Directed at self or another
    b. Irritability with mood swings over small things
    c. Guilt feelings: What did I do wrong?
    d. Wanting to hurt the one who left us

3. Bargaining
    a. God, if I do this, will you cause that to happen?
    b. Please, God: I'll do better if you change
4. Depression
    a. Emptiness, loss of meaning, sadness, sorrow
    b. Forgetfulness, aimless wandering, inability to concentrate
    c. Overeating, undereating
    d. Crying often and unexpectedly
    e. Physical complaints
    f. Isolation, apathy, loneliness
    g. Feelings of losing control
    h. Anxiety about the future
5. Acceptance
    a. Hope comes through
    b. We affirm the reality of our new situation
    c. Fear leaves
    d. We start to move forward again

Grieving is a process that you allow yourself to go through in order to get past your pain. Your passage through grief may differ, but if the shock and or denial phase continues for weeks, you may need professional assistance to move forward and begin facing reality.

No one goes through the grieving process perfectly from stages 1-5. You can bounce back and forth between states dealing with issues until you come to complete acceptance and stay there. You can get to the acceptance stage and then, leave it briefly, but you would now know what acceptance feels like. The important thing is to provide and allow time to feel and grieve; trusting in God to move you along. In your culture, you may not have been taught how to grieve or how to support others who grieve. Most individuals try "Band-Aid therapy," which is well meant but causes isolation and gives the message that the person should not feel what they are feeling. It sounds like this: "Why are you crying? Don't you know you need faith in God?" or "OK, time to get moving again."

Use the following to allow the grieving process to take place at a healthy pace for yourself or others.

DO'S	DON'TS
Be available to listen, not give unwanted advice. Find others that will do this for you.	Don't avoid your grieving friend.
	Don't say how they or you should feel.
Do encourage others to be patient with themselves. Be patient with yourself.	Don't say you know how they feel.
	Don't say that they (or you) should be grateful for what happened.
Do be available to run errands or just spend time with them and ask others to do also, for you.	
	Don't say, "You should be feeling better by now." Instead, ask how you can support them.
Allow others to express as much grief as they are feeling and are willing to share. Allow yourself to do the same.	

Jesus grieved. As He was entering Jerusalem, He wept over the city (Luke 19:41). Before His arrest in the garden of Gethsemane, Jesus said to His disciples, "My soul is exceedingly sorrowful, even to death. Stay here and watch with Me." (Matthew 26:38) Luke 22:44 tells us that, "being in agony, He prayed more earnestly. Then His sweat became like great drops of blood falling to the ground." Jesus had emotions and took them all to God. He had grief so heavy it was almost death inside Him.

He can relate to you and is your example of how to handle your grief. Hopefully, your friends will not be as the disciples were, who slept when Jesus asked for companionship. No matter what, know that Jesus sympathizes with your weaknesses and grief, for He "was in all points tempted as we [you] are, yet without sin. Let us, therefore, come boldly to the throne of grace that we may obtain mercy and find grace to help in time of need" (Hebrews 4:15-16; cf. Hebrews 2: 14-18).

GOAL SETTING

Many individuals have never been taught about goal setting. This exercise will teach you how to clearly state your goals and then set up subgoals (activities) to achieve them.

First—why should you set goals? Isn't God supposed to do everything for you? He can intervene and move you where He wants you to be, can't He? So, why do you have to do anything?

Yes, God can move you if He so desires to work that way. Most often, He doesn't. He can speak to you, but it is up to you to act as His vessel here on earth. Setting goals can be for any part of your life; for what God has spoken to your heart for you to do, for your own growth, education, or fun.

When goals are set, there's something that will arise in you to begin working to complete the goal. A purpose will grow within you and just skimming along in life doing who knows what, ends. Goals don't have to be great feats, but as you begin setting goals and moving forward, God directs your path. You can direct a moving car, but not a parked car. Goals help you get moving!

Think of the term SMARTER to support you in writing your goals:

    Specific (make it simple and clear)

    Measurable

    Achievable

    Realistic

    Timely

    Evaluate

Reset goal

Sample Goal:

I will study my Bible 4 times a week for 1 hour over a one-month period, in June.

S:	personal Bible study
M:	4 times/week
A:	clearly stated
R:	can be achieved
T:	over a month's time (specify which month)
E:	to be done after a month's time or throughout the month
R:	select another month or pick different Bible study goals

Subgoals (or activities) are those behaviors or specific activities you must do to achieve your expected end. In the example above, some activities might include:

- setting the alarm earlier
- choose the place and time for Bible study
- not planning anything else for that time frame
- turning phones and TVs off

You can be as creative as you want to be.

On the following pages, write down goals that you want to incorporate in your life and the subgoals or activities needed to achieve them, using the SMARTER way of setting goals.

A Way Of Life

LIFE DOMAIN GOALS

Life Domains (adjust the following to your needs)

SPIRITUAL GOALS: **Activities**

HEALTH AND FITNESS: **Activities**

JOB: **Activities**

EDUCATION: Activities

SOCIAL/FAMILY: Activities

RECREATION: Activities

FINANCIAL: Activities

List an area of your life and write down where you see God leading you in that area within the next year, 5 years and 10 years. You can repeat this with any area of your life. If you do not have any direction right now, seek the Lord and begin to make plans but be ever watchful in case you are going off His path for you. He will let you know and guide you as you move out. Proverbs 16:9 states, "A man's heart plans his way, but the Lord directs his steps." Proverb 16:3 promises, that when you "commit your works to the Lord, your thoughts will be established." How wonderful to know that He will give you clear and solid thoughts as you trust and obey Him!

Area:

1 year:

5 years:

10 years:

BIBLIOGRAPHY

Andrews, Andy. (2002). The Traveler's Gift. Tennessee: Thomas Nelson, Inc.

Beattie, Melody. (1987). Codependent No More. New York: Harper & Row.

Bender, Stephanie & Keleher, Kathleen. (1991). PMS—A Positive Program to Gain Control. New York: The Body Press.

Bennett, Dennis & Rita. (1971). The Holy Spirit and You. New Jersey: Logos International.

Berkhof, Louis. (1933). Manual of Christian Doctrine. Michigan: William B. Eerdmans Publishing Company.

Bradshaw, John. (1988). The Family. Florida: Health Communications, Inc.

Bridges, Jerry. (1978). The Pursuit of Holiness. Colorado: Navpress.

Bridges, Jerry. (1983). The Practice of Godliness. Colorado: Navpress.

Buhler, Rich. (1988). Pain and Pretending. Tennessee: Thomas Nelson, Inc.

Burkett, Larry. (1990). The Financial Planning Workbook. Chicago: Moody Press.

Campbell, Roderick. (1954). Israel and the New Covenant. Pennsylvania: Presbyterian and Reformed Publishing Company.

Cloud, H., & Townsend, J. (1992). Boundaries. Michigan: Zondervan Publishing House.

Corey, Gerald F. (1977). Theory and Practice of Counseling and Psychotherapy (2nd ed.). California: Wadsworth.

Dileo, Sandy. (1984). "Stress Management". California: Author.

Edman, V. Raymond. (1948). The Disciplines of Life. Minnesota: World Wide Publication.

Elwell, Walter A. (Editor). (1989). Evangelical Commentary on the Bible. Michigan: Baker Book House.

Engstrom, Ted W. (1976). The Making of a Christian Leader. Michigan: Zondervan Publishing House.

Erickson, Millard J. (1985). Christian Theology. Michigan: Baker Book House.

Esses, Michael. (1974). The Phenomenon of Obedience. New Jersey: Logos International.

Felber, Terry. (2002), Am I Making Myself Clear? Nashville: Thomas Nelson.

Foster, Richard. (1992). Prayer—Finding the Heart's True Home. California: Harper.

Fromm, Erich. (1956). The Art of Loving. New York: Harper & Row.

Green, Michael. (1975). I Believe in the Holy Spirit. Michigan: Wm. B. Eerdmans Publishing Company.

Hammond, Frank & Ida. (1973). Pigs In The Parlor. Missouri: Impact Books.

Hart, S.L. (1968). Lifetime of Love. Mass: Daughters of St. Paul.

Johnson, Spencer, MD. (1998). Who Moved My Cheese? USA: Penguin Group.

Lancaster, Wade & Jeanette. (1982). "Rational Decision Making: Managing Uncertainty". Journal of Nursing Administration. Sept. 1982. pgs. 23-28.

Leman, Dr. Kevin. (1981). Sex Begins in the Kitchen. California: Regal Books.

MacNutt, Francis, O.P. (1974). Healing. Indiana: Ave Maria Press.

Martin, Dr. Walter. (1962). Essential Christianity. California: GL Publications.

Martin, Francis P. (1979). Hung by the Tongue. Louisiana: F.P.M. Publications.

Maxwell, John C. (2023). The 16 Undeniable Laws of Communication. Maxwell Leadership Publishing

McAll, Dr. Kenneth. (1982). Healing the Family Tree. Great Britain: Sheldon Press.

Moody, Dwight L. (1881). Secret Power. California: Regal Books.

Murphy, Dr. Ed. (1992). The Handbook for Spiritual Warfare. Tennessee: Thomas Nelson Publishers, Inc.

Nutrition Search, Inc. (1973). Nutrition Almanac. New York: McGraw-Hill Book Company.

Payne, Leanne. (1991). Restoring the Christian Soul Through Healing Prayer. Illinois: Crossway Books.

Peck, M. Scott, MD. (1978). The Road Less Traveled. New York: Simon & Schuster, Inc.

Peck, M. Scott, MD. (1983). People of the Lie. New York: Simon & Schuster, Inc.

Penner, Clifford & Joyce. (1981). The Gift of Sex. Texas: Word, Inc.

Powell, John. (1969). Why Am I Afraid to Tell You Who I Am?. Illinois: Argus Communications.

Powell, John. (1974). The Secret of Staying in Love. Texas: Argus Communications.

Powell, John. (1976). Fully Human, Fully Alive. Illinois: Argus Communications.

Powell, John. (1978). Unconditional Love. Texas: Argus Communications.

Ross, Elisabeth Kübler-. (1960). On Death & Dying. Simon & Schuster/Touchstone.

Sanders, J. Oswald. (1967). Spiritual Leadership. Illinois: Moody Bible Institute.

Schaeffer, Francis A. (1971). True Spirituality. Illinois: Tyndale House Publishers.

Seamands, David A. (1981). Healing for Damaged Emotions. Illinois: SP Publications, Inc.

Smalley, Gary & Trent, John, Ph.D. (1986). The Blessing. Tennessee: Thomas Nelson, Inc.

Smalley, Gary & Trent, John, Ph.D. (1988). The Language of Love. California: Focus on the Family.

Smalley, Gary & Trent, John, Ph.D. (1990). The Two Sides of Love. Colorado: Focus on the Family.

Smith, Chuck. (1980). Effective Prayer Life. California: The Word for Today.

Swindoll, Charles R. (1983). Dropping Your Guard. New York: Bantam Books.

Taylor, Richard Shelley. (1962). The Disciplined Life. Minnesota: Bethany House Publishers.

Torrey, R.A. (1974 revised edition). The Person & Work of the Holy Spirit. Michigan: Zondervan Publishing House.

Vine, W. E. (1981). Vine's Expository Dictionary of Old and New Testament Words. New Jersey: Fleming H. Revell Company.

Watson, David. (1980). The Hidden Battle. Illinois: Harold Shaw Publishers.

White, Tom. (1993). Breaking Strongholds: How Spiritual Warfare Sets Captives Free. Michigan: Servant Publications.

Whitfield, Charles L., M.D. (1987). Healing the Child Within. Florida: Health Communications, Inc.

Wilkerson, David & Sherrill, John & Elizabeth. (1963). The Cross and The Switchblade. New Jersey: Spire Books.

Wilkerson, David. (1972). The Pocket Promise Book. California: Regal Books.

Williams, Dr. Roger J. (1971). Nutrition Against Disease. New York: Pitman Publishing Corporation.

ABOUT THE AUTHOR

My heart's cry is one of freedom and abundance for you, who read this. I was born and raised in the Panama Canal Zone and accepted Jesus Christ as my Lord and Savior between the ages of 10-13. During my childhood, God called me off by myself to spend time with Him reading His Word, next to the sparkling blue Caribbean water. He was my teacher and even with that, many mistakes did I make! When I was 17, He called me to be a Registered Nurse and it was during one of my areas of work that an earlier edition of this book was born.

I married at 22 to an unbeliever, was divorced at 30 and went through what I call baptism by fire during my first marriage. God had me clean up all I was doing that was unloving nor supporting my marriage regardless of what my ex-husband was or was not doing. Doing what is right because it is right, is the right thing to do though it's not easy. Especially when my own needs were not being met! The earlier edition of this book was completed during this season of life and I began teaching these kingdom principles of living a victorious life in the community for many years.

During the writing process, there were many times that I stopped as I did not know what the next step was. I sought the Lord and He answered me through a sense of knowing. Only then did I move on and continued this journey. One summer, I remember sitting at my desk while the sun was shining brightly on the deep-colored greenery outside my window. I looked at everyone playing while I sat working with the sun playing on the leaves. I chose to not get up and play because, above all else, my heart's cry is one of freedom and abundance for you who read this. Even then, I knew that to create something requires sacrifice and I knew that I would either get my reward later or maybe never. And the reward didn't even matter. What was and still is important, is that I finish the work I promised God I would and was called to do.

I have since remarried, have a wonderful family and look forward to more of God's blessings in my life as I give to others! May you ask Him for your way and follow it. Therein is fulfillment and blessings galore. Why else are we to be here but to live out what was ordained for each of us from the beginning of time? That is why this work was written. That is why this work was written for you.

> With blessings always,

> *Nancy Williams*

www.ingramcontent.com/pod-product-compliance
Lightning Source LLC
Chambersburg PA
CBHW060404050426
42449CB00009B/1895